GOLD experience

2ND EDITION

A2
Key for Schools

EXAM PRACTICE

CONTENTS

EXAM OVERVIEW

Cambridge English Qualification A2 Key for Schools Exam, otherwise known as **Cambridge Key for Schools**, is an examination set at **A2 level** of the Common European Framework of Reference for Languages (CEFR). It is made up of **three papers**, each testing a different area of ability in English: Reading and Writing, Listening, and Speaking.

Reading and Writing	1 hour	50% of the marks
Listening	35 minutes (approximately)	25% of the marks
Speaking	8–10 minutes for each pair of students (approximately)	25% of the marks

All the examination questions are task-based. Rubrics (instructions) are important and candidates should read them carefully. They set the context and give important information about the tasks. There are separate answer sheets for recording answers for the Reading and Writing paper and the Listening paper.

Paper	Format	Task focus
Reading and Writing Seven Parts 32 questions	**Part 1: three-option multiple choice.** Reading six short texts and choosing the correct answer.	**Part 1:** reading short texts for the main idea, detail, and writer's purpose.
	Part 2: matching. Reading three short texts or paragraphs on the same topic and matching the correct text or paragraph to the question.	**Part 2:** reading for detailed understanding.
	Part 3: three-option multiple choice. Five multiple-choice questions.	**Part 3:** reading for main idea(s), detail, opinion, attitude and writer's purpose.
	Part 4: three-option multiple-choice cloze. Reading a text with six gaps and selecting the correct word to complete each gap.	**Part 4:** reading and identifying appropriate words.
	Part 5: open cloze. Short text with six gaps. Completing the text with one word in each gap.	**Part 5:** reading and writing appropriate words to fill in the gaps.
	Part 6: guided writing; writing a short message. Reading an email or reading about a situation and writing an email.	**Part 6:** Writing an email to a friend including three pieces of information. 25 words or more
	Part 7: guided writing; writing a short narrative. Three pictures which show a story.	**Part 7:** Writing the short story shown in the three pictures. 35 words or more
Listening Five Parts 25 questions	**Part 1: three-option multiple choice.** Listening to five short dialogues and choosing the correct picture for each answer.	**Part 1:** listening to identify key information.
	Part 2: gap fill. Listening to a longer monologue and writing the missing word, number, date or time in five gaps.	**Part 2:** listening and writing down information.
	Part 3: three-option multiple choice. Listening to a longer dialogue and choosing the correct answer to five questions.	**Part 3:** listening to identify key information, feelings and opinions.
	Part 4: three-option multiple choice. Listening to five short dialogues or monologues and choosing the correct answer for each text-based question.	**Part 4:** listening for gist, main idea or topic.
	Part 5: matching. Listening to a longer dialogue and matching five questions with seven options. An example is given.	**Part 5:** listening to identify specific information.
Speaking Two Parts	**Part 1: interview:** examiner-led conversation. 3-4 minutes	**Part 1:** giving personal information.
	Part 2: collaborative task: two-way conversation with visual prompt. Examiner asks two more questions to broaden the topic. 5-6 minutes	**Part 2:** asking and answering simple questions, expressing likes and dislikes and giving reasons.

PRACTICE TEST 1 WITH GUIDANCE

About the Reading and Writing test

The test lasts 60 minutes and there are seven parts. Parts 1–5 are reading tasks. Parts 6–7 are writing tasks.

You read both short and longer texts and answer different types of questions.

- In Parts 1–4, you have to show that you can read and completely understand the texts.

- In Part 5, you have to both read the text and show that you can use language correctly.

Parts 1–4: Reading

What do I do in Part 1?
In Part 1, you read six short texts on different topics. Some of the texts are notices you might see at school or in other places. Others might be messages, such as emails, text messages, etc.

There is one multiple-choice question about each text. You have to choose from three options the answer which is closest to the meaning of the text.

How is Part 2 different to Part 1?
In Part 2, you read three short texts or one longer text divided into three paragraphs. This time, the texts or paragraphs are all on the same topic and contain similar ideas and information.

The texts are usually about people. You have to decide which text or paragraph a question is about. For example, you might need to decide which person was taught to cook by one of his family.

What do I do in Part 3?
In Part 3, you read one longer text. This is usually an article about an interesting person, event or place to visit. You have to answer five three-option multiple-choice questions about the text to show that you can understand the detailed meaning, as well as what the writer is saying about the topic.

How is Part 4 different to Part 3?
In Part 4, you have to read one text on a topic. Six words are missing from the text. For each missing word, there is a multiple-choice question, which gives you three possible words to use in the gap. You have to choose the best word. You look at the words before and after the gap to help you choose the best one. In this way, you show your understanding of the text, of vocabulary and how words are used together in a text.

Part 5: Reading

What do I do in Part 5?
In Part 5, you also have to read one or two short texts with six words missing. There is an example at the beginning (0). This time, however, you have to find the missing word yourself – there are none to choose from. In this part, the missing words are mostly grammatical words like pronouns, prepositions, etc.

By choosing the correct word, you show that you understand how to use grammatical words to write good sentences.

Parts 6 and 7: Writing

How many things do I have to write?
You must write two pieces in the Reading and Writing test.

- The first is always a short message, usually an **email** (Part 6).

- The second is a story (Part 7). You look at three pictures and write the story shown in the pictures.

What do I do in Part 6?
In Part 6, on the page you will read an email or read about a situation.

The email is from a friend, and your friend asks you three questions. Your task is to write an email replying to this friend, answering all three questions.

The situation explains what a friend needs to know about, for example, a class project. There are three points or pieces of information that you must give your friend. Your task is to write an email giving your friend all three pieces of information.

You should write 25 words or more.

What do I do in Part 7?
In Part 7, you must write a story.

On the page, you will see three pictures. Your task is to write the **story** shown in the pictures. You should describe what you see in the pictures and link them together.

How much time do I get to do the test?

You have about twenty minutes to do the Writing test. That includes the time to think before you start writing, and the time to check what you have written.

How many marks do I get for each part?

You get the same number of marks in Part 1 and in Part 2, so you must try to do both well.

The examiner will give you good marks if:

- you have included all the information;

- your writing is clear and easy to follow and understand;

- you have used some good language, with good spelling and punctuation.

How do I do the Writing test?

Look at the **Tip strips** next to each task. They will show you how to do the task, step by step.

Part 1

Questions 1 – 6

For each question, choose the correct answer.

1

> Special pizzas all €15
> Today's special:
> hot chilli
> Extra cheese: €1
> (usual price)

A The hot chilli pizza includes extra cheese.

B The special pizza is cheaper than usual today.

C The price is higher if you want more cheese on your pizza.

TIP STRIP

Question 1: How much will you pay if you want a hot chilli pizza with extra cheese?

Question 2: What should you do to find out more information?

Question 3: Where is Ted going tonight – and who is travelling with him?

Question 4: When is the artist coming? And when must students speak to Mrs Johnson? What about?

Question 5: Where can you *always* buy tickets at the station?

Question 6: Who first arranged to collect Gemma from the cinema? And what's going to happen now?

2

FOR SALE

Playbox games machine €50. Also, several games – phone for titles and prices. 07845 60576863

A If you get the games machine, you can have some games for free.

B Ring this number if you want to know how much the games cost.

C You can't have the games if you don't buy the machine as well.

3

Jacob,

My dad can drive me to football practice at school tonight on his way to the swimming club – so do you want a lift?

Ted

A Ted is offering to take Jacob to football practice tonight.

B Ted is letting Jacob know where football practice is tonight.

C Ted is asking Jacob if he prefers swimming instead of football practice tonight.

4

To: Art students

From: Mrs Johnson

Students who want to meet the artist coming to our school next week must give me their names by Friday.

A People studying art must go and meet an artist at their school next week.

B Students who don't tell Mrs Johnson by Friday can't meet the artist visiting their school.

C Mrs Johnson still has places available to meet an artist at school this Friday.

5

STATION

This ticket machine isn't working.

Please use another machine or go to ticket office.

A You have to go to the ticket office to buy tickets today.

B There are only machines available for you to buy tickets at this station.

C If you can't find an available machine, buy your tickets at the office.

6

Gemma,
Sorry – I've got to work late tonight, so Dad will pick you up after the cinema instead of me. Have a lovely time!
Mum

A There's been a change of plan about Gemma's cinema trip tonight.

B Gemma can't get home after the cinema tonight.

C Gemma's father is delayed at work, so her mum's collecting her from the cinema.

Part 2

Questions 7 – 13

For each question, choose the correct answer.

		Sam	Ben	Karl
7	Which person was taught to cook by one of his family?	A	B	C
8	Which person thinks his family don't always give their true opinion about his food?	A	B	C
9	Which person makes new dishes of his own?	A	B	C
10	Which person likes cooking difficult dishes?	A	B	C
11	Which person prepares meals for people who can't eat some things?	A	B	C
12	Which person likes cooking for himself before he leaves home each day?	A	B	C
13	Which person can't think of one dish he likes more than any others?	A	B	C

TIP STRIP

You may find similar information in more than one text but only one will be correct.

Question 7: Each text mentions *family* but which person was taught to cook by someone?

Question 9: Which person talks about making food by *putting things in a pan*?

Question 10: Who talks about dishes that are *hard to make*? Does he like making them?

Question 12: Which meal do you have in the morning, before you leave home? Which person talks about this?

Question 13: Who doesn't have one dish that he likes best?

Three teenagers talk about cooking

Sam

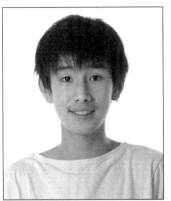

I'm not sure I've got a favourite dish, but there are things I like cooking. My family's from China and the dishes we have can be hard to make. I enjoy trying, to learn the right way to make them, instead of doing the same meals every day. I've got a great cookbook I use, which my grandmother gave me. I sometimes cook for the whole family and they say they like my food – but I think they're just trying to be nice!

Ben

There aren't many things I can cook well, but when I'm hungry I can make pasta, which my friends really enjoy too. I learnt how to make that and other dishes just by watching my mum. But she also showed me the best way to make them. Our family's always been a bit difficult to cook for, because some of us don't like meat and others aren't able to have milk or cheese. But that's OK because I enjoy making the simple dishes that we can share together.

Karl

My family all enjoy cooking and they're good at it – my dad makes great burgers! But I prefer to cook what I like, and sometimes I just put different things into the pan and see what happens! It's not always successful, so I don't share it with my family but I like doing it – and I always eat what I've made. I enjoy making myself a good breakfast – toast and eggs. I'm ready for anything after that!

Part 3

Questions 14 – 18

For each question, choose the correct answer.

Going climbing!

By Claire Green, age 12

As a child, I always loved climbing – trees, walls, anything! I just loved being high up. But what I really wanted was to go into the mountains, so on my 14th birthday my dad gave me a surprise present – a climbing trip with him!

We've been climbing many times since then, and usually go into the mountains near our home. We don't do difficult climbs, but we always want to get near the top if possible. We have to carry all our equipment with us. We usually go for a day, and don't take tents, so luckily my bag is quite light. Anyway, the views are always amazing.

When I'm climbing, I need to think hard about what I'm doing, so there's no time to worry about schoolwork or things like that. Instead, I enjoy just thinking about where to put my hands and feet to stay safe and not fall – and how soon we'll have our picnic lunch, my favourite part of the day! Climbing always makes me really hungry.

We try to climb only when the weather's good, and on our last climb, it was a warm, sunny day when we left. However, the wind became stronger and colder as we climbed higher, and sometimes I felt I just couldn't keep climbing. Later, it began to rain, so I was glad when Dad said we should go back down the mountain. And when we got to the bottom, we had some hot chocolate – the best ever!

14   Why did Claire go on her first climbing trip into the mountains?

    A   She wanted to try a new hobby.

    B   She asked for it as a birthday present.

    C   She was taken there by her dad.

15   Claire says that on her climbing trips with her dad

    A   they need to carry heavy equipment.

    B   they usually camp in the mountains.

    C   they try to climb as high as they can.

16   When Claire is climbing, she

    A   worries about staying safe.

    B   is happy when they stop to eat.

    C   thinks about her homework.

17   What was the weather like on their last climb?

    A   It stayed fine all day.

    B   It changed during their trip.

    C   It was wet when they started.

18   How did Claire feel during the last climb?

    A   She didn't mind when they decided not to finish it.

    B   She was sad that they couldn't go any further.

    C   She was pleased at how far they climbed.

Part 4

Questions 19 – 24

For each question, choose the correct answer.

Arctic hares

Have you ever seen an Arctic hare? It **(19)** .... to the same family as the rabbit, but it's much bigger, and its ears are **(20)** .... than a rabbit's. The Arctic hare lives in very cold countries, where it's often too cold even for trees to grow, so it needs its thick coat to **(21)** .... it warm. Its coat is usually white in winter, but the colour **(22)** .... to grey in summer.

Arctic hares can grow up to 70 centimetres and are **(23)** .... very fast – they can run over 60 kilometres per hour. They usually eat plants but will also eat fish when they need to. The babies are usually born in spring, and unlike baby rabbits, they're able to see as **(24)** .... as they're born.

19	A includes	B belongs	C joins
20	A longer	B further	C higher
21	A stay	B hold	C keep
22	A becomes	B changes	C gets
23	A probably	B especially	C certainly
24	A soon	B well	C early

Questions 25 – 30

For each question, write the correct answer.
Write one word for each gap.

Example: | 0 | | A | R | E | | | | | | | | | | | | | | | | |

To:	Jake
From:	Mark
Re:	Film!

Hi Jake

How are you? I hope you're OK. **(0)** .... you free on Saturday evening? I've

downloaded a great film onto my laptop. **(25)** .... you like to come and

watch it **(26)** .... me? It's called *Star Maker*, and everyone says it's a really

good film!

My mum says that **(27)** .... you want, you could come and have something

(28) .... eat before we watch the film. We usually have dinner at around

7.00. Is that OK for you? Dad says he can take you home **(29)** .... the film.

Please let **(30)** .... know if you can come. I hope you can!

Best wishes,

Mark

TIP STRIP

Question 25: Which word do you use if you want to *invite* someone to do something – _____ you like ...?

Question 28: When you have a meal, you *have something* _____ *eat.*

Question 29: Jake's dad will take Mark home when the film finishes – so he'll take him home _____ *the film.*

Part 6

Question 31

Your friend Lee was sick on Friday and now wants to know about the class geography project.
Write an email to Lee.

Say:

- **what** he has to write about

- **how much** he has to write

- **when** he needs to complete it by.

Write **25 words** or more.

Question 32

Look at the three pictures.
Write the story shown in the pictures.
Write **35 words** or more.

TIP STRIP

Look carefully at the pictures. What's happening in each one? Here are some key words to help you write the story: *cycle, lake, sunny, sunglasses, hat, fall off, surprised, pick up, wet, sad.*

GUIDANCE: LISTENING

About the Listening test

The Listening paper lasts about 35 minutes. This includes six minutes for you to write your answers on the Answer Sheet. There are five Parts in the Listening test. In Parts 1 and 4, you hear short recordings and answer one question with three options on each recording. In Part 2, you hear one long recording and you have to write down five pieces of information.

In Part 3, you hear a long recording and you have to answer five three-option multiple-choice questions. In Part 5, you have to answer five matching questions. You hear each recording twice.

How to do the test

What do I do in Part 1?

You hear five different short recordings and you have to answer a question about each one. You always hear two people talking about something in an everyday situation.

For each question, there are three pictures. You read the question, listen to the recording and decide which picture is the correct answer. The questions are mostly about information like times, places, prices, what people like best or what people decide to do.

Listen carefully, because you hear about the things in all three pictures, but only one picture answers the question.

What do I do in Part 2?

In Part 2, there is one long recording and there is always just one person talking. For example, you may hear a teacher giving her class some information.

You hear a sentence that tells you who is speaking and what they're talking about. You then have time to read a set of notes from which some of the information is missing. Read this carefully and think about the type of information you need to fill each of the five gaps.

When you listen, follow the information in the task. You will hear some of the words that are written there. Be ready to write the missing information in the gaps. Write the exact word, number, date or time that you hear.

Always listen carefully. You may hear more than one word that could fit in a gap. Sometimes, you have to write the spelling of a word, like somebody's name for example. Listen to the letters carefully.

What do I do in Part 3?

Part 3, there is also one long recording, but this time it's a conversation between two people. You hear and read a sentence that tells you who is speaking and what they are talking about.

For example, it could be two friends talking about a concert they have just been to. You then have time to read the five three-option multiple-choice questions. The information in the recording comes in the same order as the questions.

You listen and choose the correct answer (A, B, C). Listen carefully and think about the meaning of what the people say. You may not always hear the same words that are written in the options, but you do hear the answer to the question.

How is Part 4 different from Part 1?

There are five different recordings like in Part 1 but there may be two people speaking or only one.

There's one question about each recording, but this time it's a written multiple-choice question. You hear a sentence that tells who is speaking and what they are talking about. Then you have time to read the question and the options (A, B, C). You listen and choose the correct answer.

You need to listen for the main idea or topic. You do not usually hear the same words that you read in the options, so think about the meaning of what the people are saying.

Some questions ask about one of the people, but others may ask about both. Sometimes the question might ask, for example, why someone didn't go somewhere or didn't buy something. Always read the question carefully.

What do I have to do in Part 5?

In Part 5, you hear one long recording and you have to match questions to answers. There are always two people speaking.

There are five questions and seven options. There is an example at the beginning so you see eight options, A–H, on the page.

You hear and read a sentence that tells you who is speaking and what they are talking about, for example, it may be a boy telling a friend about the postcards he got from different people.

You listen and choose the correct answer (A–H). Listen carefully and think about the meaning of what the people say. You may not always hear the same words that are written in the options. Sometimes you may hear two words that are options but only one answers the question correctly.

Part I

Questions 1 – 5

For each question, choose the correct picture.

1 Which one is Anna's school?

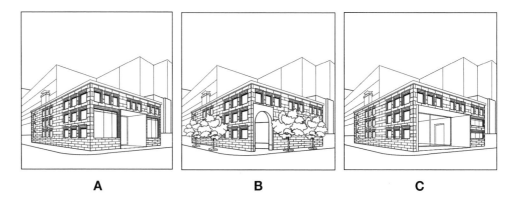

A   B   C

2 When does the football match start?

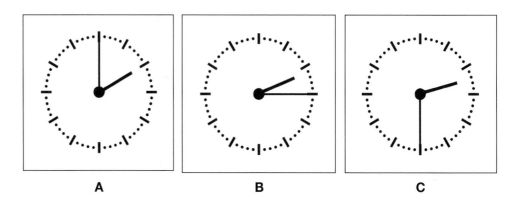

A   B   C

3 Which size trainers does the boy decide to get?

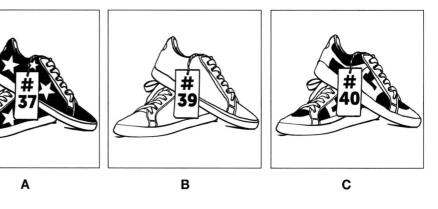

A   B   C

4 Where did the girl eat lunch yesterday?

A   **B**   **C**

5 What has the boy just bought?

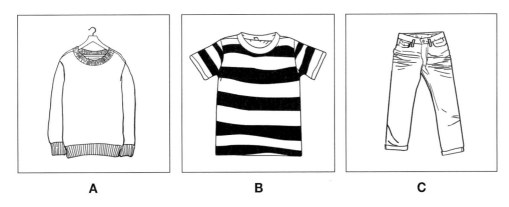

A   **B**   **C**

Part 2

Questions 6 – 10

For each question, write the correct answer in the gap.

Write **one word**, or **a number** or **a date** or **a time**.

You will hear a teacher talking to her students about a school cycle ride.

School Cycle Ride

Day of cycle ride: *Saturday*

How far the ride will be: **(6)** .... kms

Where the ride will finish: **(7)** ....

What's important to bring: **(8)** ....

What to check on the bike: **(9)** ....

What everyone will get at the end: **(10)** ....

Part 3

Questions 11 – 15

For each question, choose the correct answer.

___

You will hear Henry talking to his friend Marta about a concert they have just been to.

11   Why did Henry want to go to the concert?

    A   His favourite band was playing.

    B   He enjoys listening to rock music.

    C   He was told about it by a friend.

12   Marta thinks the guitar player

    A   sang very well.

    B   was too loud.

    C   played the best.

13   Marta was sad that she couldn't

    A   have a chat with the band.

    B   buy a poster of the band.

    C   get a photo of the band.

14   Their tickets cost

    A   €18.

    B   €19.75.

    C   €25.50.

15   How will they get home?

    A   They'll walk.

    B   They'll go in Henry's dad's car.

    C   They'll catch a bus.

TIP STRIP

Before the recording starts, quickly read through the questions. You'll hear a *cue* for each question – like *tickets* for Qu 14 – so that you don't lose your place during the recording.

Question 13: Marta says something was *a shame* – so was she happy or sad about it?

Question 14: Henry and Marta got a *discount* – so were their tickets cheaper or more expensive than normal?

Question 15: What does Henry say about his dad tonight? And what *goes to our street*?

Part 4

Questions 16 – 20

For each question, choose the correct answer.

---

16   You will hear two friends talking about subjects they study at school.
Which one does the boy like the best?

     A   maths

     B   art

     C   biology

17   You will hear a girl phoning a friend about a story competition she's entered.
How does she feel about the competition?

     A   surprised that so many people entered

     B   worried that her story won't be good enough

     C   happy that her teacher liked her story

TIP STRIP

You will hear five *different* conversations, so be ready each time to listen to the recording for the next question.

Question 16: Which subject does the boy want to *study ... every day?*

Question 17: The girl says 'I didn't think that would happen!' What does she mean?

Question 19: What does *below zero* mean? Is it very warm or very cold?

18   You will hear a boy talking to a shop assistant about a sweater.
What does he want to buy?

     A   a cheaper sweater

     B   a darker sweater

     C   a bigger sweater

19   You will hear a girl talking about her holiday by the sea.
Why didn't she go swimming?

     A   The weather wasn't good.

     B   The water wasn't the right temperature.

     C   The beach was very crowded.

20   You will hear a girl talking about something that she's lost.
What has she lost?

     A   her phone

     B   her train ticket

     C   her bag

Part 5

Questions 21 – 25

For each question, choose the correct answer.

You will hear Paolo talking to Maria about his picture postcards. Who sent him each postcard?

Example:

0   brother   ☐ *F*

People		**Pictures on the postcards**	
21	sister ☐	**A**	a beach
		B	a campsite
22	friend ☐	**C**	a castle
		D	a forest
23	grandparents ☐	**E**	a house
		F	a lake
24	cousin ☐	**G**	a mountain
25	uncle ☐	**H**	a ship

TIP STRIP

You will hear the *names* of the people in order, so listen carefully for what comes next. Which postcard did they send?

Question 21: Where was his sister's hotel? *In the middle* of what?

Question 22: Where could you go *climbing*? Look carefully at the list.

Question 23: When they're talking about Paolo's grandparents, you'll hear a *distractor* – a word in the list that isn't the key. Which word is it?

TEST
1

LISTENING

LISTENING **TEST 1**   25

GUIDANCE: SPEAKING

About the Speaking test

The *Speaking* paper lasts between 8 and 10 minutes and there are two Parts.

There are two examiners; one speaks to you and the other one just listens. You do the test with a partner. In some parts you talk to the examiner, and in other parts you talk to each other.

How many marks do I get for each part?

The examiners give you marks for the test as a whole. There are some marks for grammar and vocabulary, but this is only one of the things the examiners give marks for. Just as important are how well you organise your language, how clear your pronunciation is and how well you interact with your partner.

How to do the test

What do I do in Part 1?

In Part 1, the examiner asks each of you questions about yourselves. You speak to the examiner in this part, and not to each other. The first few questions are simple ones, for example, your name, your age and where you come from. You just give short simple answers to these questions.

After this, the examiner asks each of you more questions on everyday topics, for example, ways of travelling or what you do at the weekend. You only need to give short answers to these questions but the examiner will ask each of you a question which starts *Please tell me something about* … and you should give a longer answer to this question.

How is Part 2 different to Part 1?

In Part 2, you speak to each other. The examiner gives you a page with five pictures on it, for example, showing different TV programmes. The examiner asks you if you like or don't like these things or these activities. You talk together saying if you like or don't like these things or activities. You should give your reasons.

The examiner then asks some questions about some or all of the pictures, for example, if you think the thing or activity is interesting, exciting, boring, etc.

Finally, the examiner asks each of you two more questions on the same topic. You should give reasons for your answers.

Part I (3–4 minutes)

Phase I

The examiner will ask you and your partner some questions about yourself.

To both candidates	Good morning / afternoon / evening.
	I'm ...., and this is ....
(*Candidate A*)	What's your name?
(*Candidate B*)	And what's your name?

Extra help questions

Are you from (Spain, etc.)?
Do you live in … (name of district / town, etc.)?

(*Candidate A*)
B, how old are you? ....
Where do you come from? ....
Where do you live?

Thank you.

(*Candidate B*)
A, how old are you? ....
Where do you come from? ....
Where do you live?

Thank you.

Are you from (Spain, etc.)?
Do you live in … (name of district / town, etc.)?

TIP STRIP

- **What's your name?** My name is ....
- **How old are you?** I'm .... years old.
- **Where do you come from?** I come from / I'm from …(which country? How do you say the country in English?)
- **Where do you live?** I live in … (You can say the name of your village, town or city.)

Part I (continued)

Phase 2

Now, let's talk about **ways of travelling.**

A, how do you get to school every day? ....
And, is it a good way to travel? ....

B, how do you travel around your city, town
or village?
And, how easy is it to travel around? ....

Extended response
Now, **A**, please tell me something about
your favourite way of travelling.

Extra help questions

Do you travel to school by bus?
Do you enjoy your journey?

Do you cycle around your city, town
or village?
Is it easy to travel around your city, town or village?

When do you walk in your city, town or village?
Does anyone in your family have a car?
Have you travelled by train or plane this year?

TIP STRIP

Travelling

A By car, bus, train or bike? On foot?
   Is the journey difficult? Fun? Crowded? What do you do during your journey?
B Can you cycle, walk, or go by bus, train or car?
   Think about: easy / difficult / expensive? Does it take a long time?

Extended response

Do you love travelling by train? Plane? Car? Bus?
Do you prefer walking? Why?
Think about: fun / comfortable / exciting /
interesting / fast?

Now, let's talk about **friends.**

B, when do you usually see your friends? ....
And, where do you go with your friends? ....

A, what do you do with friends after school? ....
And when do you usually go to a friend's house? ....

Extended response
Now, **B**, tell me something about your
best friend.

Extra help questions

Do you see your friends every day?
Do you go to the park?

Do you meet your friends after school?
Do you sometimes go to a friend's house?

Is your best friend in your class?
Does your best friend live near you?
Where did you first meet your best friend?

TIP STRIP

Friends

B every day / at school / in the evenings / at the weekends?
   Do you: go shopping / to the park / to the cinema / to a sports centre / to the
   swimming pool?
A go to a café / go to the library / go to an after-school club / play a sport /
   watch TV?
   Going to a friend's house: in the evenings / after school / at the weekends?

Extended response

Talk about your best friend, e.g. boy or girl / age /
where you met / when you see him or her / why
you like your friend / what you do together

Phase 1 (3–4 minutes)

Now, in this part of the test, you are going to talk together.

[Turn to the pictures on page 50]

Here are some pictures that show **different TV programmes**.

Do you like these different kinds of TV programmes? Say why or why not.

I'll say that again. Do you like these different kinds of TV programmes?
Say why or why not.

All right? Now, talk together.

🕐 *1–2 minutes*

The examiner will ask you at least one question each:

Do you think ...
... quiz programmes are interesting?
... sports programmes are exciting?
... news programmes are important?
... comedy programmes are funny?
... music programmes are boring?

> **Extra help questions**
>
> Why?/ Why not?
> What do **you** think?

So, **A**, which of these programmes do you like best?
And you, **B**, which of these programmes do you like best?

🕐 *1–2 minutes*

Thank you.

Part 2

Now, do you prefer watching TV with your family or your friends, **B**? … (Why?)

And what about you, **A**? (Do you prefer watching TV with your family or your friends?) … (Why?)

Where is your favourite place to sit and watch TV, **A**? … (Why?)

And what about you, **B**? (Where is your favourite place to sit and watch TV?) … (Why?)

🕐 *1–2 minutes*

Thank you.

That is the end of the test.

TIP STRIP

Do you prefer watching TV with your family or your friends?

Where do you like watching TV? In the living room? In the kitchen? In your bedroom? At a friend's house? At your grandparents' house?

EXAM OVERVIEW

Paper	Format
Reading and Writing Seven Parts 32 questions	**Part 1: three-option multiple choice.** Reading six short texts and choosing the correct answer.
	Part 2: matching. Reading three short texts or paragraphs on the same topic and matching the correct text or paragraph to the question.
	Part 3: three-option multiple choice. Five multiple-choice questions.
	Part 4: three-option multiple-choice cloze. Reading a text with six gaps and selecting the correct word to complete each gap.
	Part 5: open cloze. Short text with six gaps. Completing the text with one word in each gap.
	Part 6: guided writing; writing a short message. Reading an email or reading about a situation and writing an email.
	Part 7: guided writing; writing a short narrative. Three pictures which show a story.
Listening Five Parts 25 questions	**Part 1:** three-option multiple choice. Listening to five short dialogues and choosing the correct picture for each answer.
	Part 2: gap fill. Listening to a longer monologue and writing the missing word, number, date or time in five gaps.
	Part 3: three-option multiple choice. Listening to a longer dialogue and choosing the correct answer to five questions.
	Part 4: three-option multiple choice. Listening to five short dialogues or monologues and choosing the correct answer for each text-based question.
	Part 5: matching. Listening to a longer dialogue and matching five questions with seven options. An example is given.
Speaking Two Parts	**Part 1:** interview: examiner-led conversation. 3-4 minutes
	Part 2: collaborative task: two-way conversation with visual prompt. Examiner asks two more questions to broaden the topic. 5-6 minutes

Part I

Questions 1 – 6

For each question, choose the correct answer.

1

Sarah,

I didn't have my jacket when I got home on Friday. Is it at your house? Can you let me know?

Lily

A Lily isn't sure where she left something when she was at Sarah's house.

B Lily wants Sarah to come to her house and look for something.

C Lily has lost something that she thinks Sarah may have.

2

For perfect hot chocolate:
Put two spoons of chocolate into a cup, and add hot milk, or water if you prefer.

A There's only one way to make hot chocolate if you want it to be perfect.

B The best way to make hot chocolate is to use hot milk.

C You can choose to make hot chocolate in the way that you enjoy.

3

To: All students
From: Mr Hatfield

Don't forget to come and get all the project work you've done from the History Room before the end of term.

A Mr Hatfield is telling students to give him their projects before term finishes.

B Mr Hatfield wants students to take their projects home before the holiday begins.

C Mr Hatfield has collected students' projects to give back before the end of term.

4

Billy,

Your sandwiches for lunch are in the fridge – pack them in your bag. Don't forget Dad's driving you to school this morning.

Love, Mum

What is Billy's mum doing?

A telling Billy what to eat before he goes to school

B making sure Billy knows how he's getting to school today

C explaining what Billy needs to do to make sandwiches for his lunch

5

Students
No bags in library.
Leave them by front desk
– collect on way out.

A Students are asked to pick up their bags from the desk when they leave.

B There aren't any student bags available here at the moment.

C You must put your bag by the desk where you're working in the library.

6

FOR SALE
Football boots – size 38
€20
Used once
Now too small
Call Alex: 45735362

A Phone this person if you have some football boots you want to sell.

B The person who owns these boots has never worn them.

C This person isn't able to wear the football boots he's selling any more.

Part 2

Questions 7 – 13

For each question, choose the correct answer.

	Kamila	Sophie	Corinne
7 Which person enjoys the views from one building she likes?	A	B	C
8 Which person preferred the older buildings to the modern ones in her city now?	A	B	C
9 Which person doesn't like some of the unusual buildings in her city?	A	B	C
10 Which person likes exploring buildings where famous people lived?	A	B	C
11 Which person enjoys going to the top of very tall buildings?	A	B	C
12 Which person thinks some modern buildings look better after it's dark?	A	B	C
13 Which person prefers buildings that she can go inside?	A	B	C

Three girls talk about buildings in their cities

Kamila

The centre of my city has lots of tall new buildings, but they're mainly for companies to work in. And when they were built, many older buildings were lost, and I actually liked those better. In my opinion, the new ones don't look very special. They're just grey and boring. And if you go to the top, all you see is lots more tall buildings. However, at night, when all the lights are on inside, some don't look quite so bad!

Sophie

There are a few old houses near the centre of my city. They were the homes of well-known writers and artists many years ago, so it's interesting to visit them. And you can see a long way from the windows in my favourite one, because it's by the river. There are modern buildings in my city too, over 30 floors high, and they're also fun to visit. But you can't go in and look around the ones that belong to businesses, so that's a bit boring!

Corinne

There are still many old buildings in the centre of my city, and some are quite important because famous people lived there. There are lots more company buildings now too, and some are really high. So, it's fun to go in the lift, right up to the roof! But some of the newer buildings look quite strange from the outside. I guess the people who built them wanted them to look different, but I think they're quite ugly.

Questions 14 – 18

For each question, choose the correct answer.

Cycling in the snow

By Nick Jones, age 11

It usually snows once or twice in my town during the winter and the snow can bring problems. Everyone works to get the snow off the roads, so traffic keeps moving. But that doesn't always happen on the paths, so going anywhere on foot is difficult. But the local trains still keep going – so until last year, that's how I travelled to school on snowy days.

Then when it snowed last winter, I decided to cycle to school instead. It was easier than I thought because the roads weren't busy, and I never felt in danger. But people in my class couldn't believe it – they all came in cars!

Of course, I had to prepare for the trip. Luckily, I already had a warm jacket and trousers to wear. I also put special snow tyres on my bike – with some help from Dad! But he wasn't worried about me cycling in the snow – he knows I'm careful on my bike, even in good weather.

But sometimes bad things still happen. One day, I was cycling home when I saw another cyclist hit a tree. He wasn't hurt, but I was so busy watching him, I suddenly found I was on the ground! I was worried about my bike's front wheel, but it was OK.

You can still cycle quickly in the snow, but remember you'll need to use your feet to stop! And if there's ice, don't cycle on it as it's very difficult to stay on your bike!

14   Which people have problems in the writer's town when it snows?

    A   car drivers

    B   train passengers

    C   people walking

15   When Nick first cycled to school in the snow

    A   his classmates were really amazed.

    B   he was surprised there weren't many other cyclists.

    C   he thought the roads didn't feel safe.

16   To cycle to school in the snow, Nick

    A   got some special cycling clothes.

    B   made changes to his bike.

    C   cycled more carefully.

17   Nick explains that one day in the snow he

    A   fell off his bike.

    B   nearly hit a tree.

    C   broke his front wheel.

18   What advice does Nick give about cycling in the snow?

    A   Don't try to go too fast.

    B   Don't try to cycle where there's ice.

    C   Don't try to stop quickly.

Part 4

Questions 19 – 24

For each question, choose the correct answer.

The violin

Many people believe the first ever violin was made in Italy by Andrea Amati, 500 years ago. However, the most expensive violin ever was made in 1741, and would now **(19)** .... $18 million to buy!

The name violin **(20)** .... from the Latin word *vitula*. Violins can be made of over seventy **(21)** .... pieces of wood, put together to build the violin.

Some children start learning to play the violin when they are as **(22)** .... as four. At that age, they play an instrument that's a smaller **(23)** .... than an adult's violin.

The violin can be a difficult instrument to play well and playing it can be hard work. So, scientists actually think that you can get more **(24)** .... when you're playing a violin than when you go to the gym!

19	**A** earn	**B** cost	**C** pay
20	**A** begins	**B** arrives	**C** comes
21	**A** different	**B** right	**C** other
22	**A** early	**B** young	**C** soon
23	**A** size	**B** level	**C** piece
24	**A** health	**B** practice	**C** exercise

Question 25 – 30

For each question, write the correct answer.
Write one word for each gap.

Example: | 0 | | *W* | *A* | *S* | | | | | | | | | | | | | | | |

To: Emily

From: Katie

Re: Holiday

Hi Emily,

How **(0)** .... your holiday last week? I hope you **(25)** .... a good time.

I've just come back from a week **(26)** .... Auntie Jane's house. My brother

came **(27)** .... me and we really enjoyed it. Auntie Jane lives near the sea,

and the weather was really warm, **(28)** .... we tried to spend as much time

(29) .... possible on the beach.

One evening, we decided to cook dinner for Auntie Jane, but we

needed help!

(30) .... you enjoy cooking? I'm not very good at it, unfortunately.

Hope to see you soon.

Katie

Part 6

Question 31

Your friend Cary has just come to live in your town and has invited you to go shopping in the market with her.
Write an email to Cary.

In the email say:

- **when** you could go to the market with Cary

- **where** you can meet

- **what** you can buy at the market.

Write **25 words** or more.

Question 32

Look at the three pictures.
Write the story shown in the pictures.
Write **35 words** or more.

Part 1

Questions 1 – 5

For each question, choose the correct picture.

1 What was the weather like at the beach yesterday?

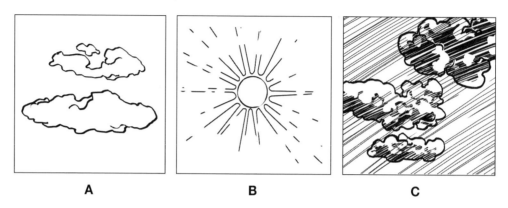

A   B   C

2 What does the girl's brother do?

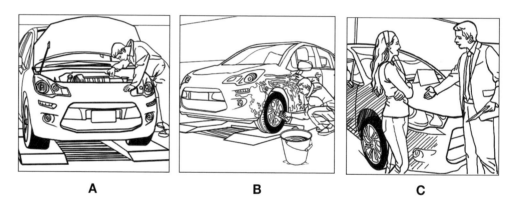

A   B   C

3 Who collected the girl from the cinema?

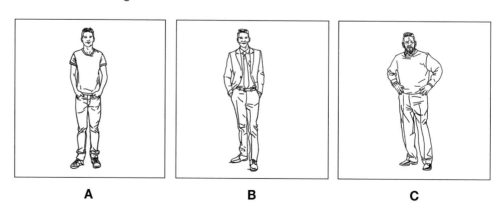

A   B   C

4   Which clothes will the boy wear to the party?

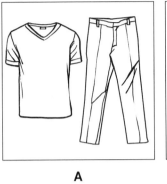

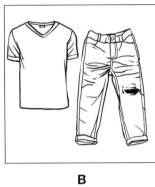

A   B   C

5   Where has the girl just been?

A   B   C

Part 2

Questions 6 – 10

For each question, write the correct answer in the gap.

Write **one word**, or **a number** or **a date** or **a time**.

You will hear a girl called Amy talking to her class about a photography exhibition she went to.

Photography Exhibition

Name of the arts centre: The *Project*

Where it is: **(6)** opposite the ....

Subject of the photos: **(7)** ....

Student ticket prices: **(8)** £...........................

Open on weekdays until: **(9)** ....

Website address: **(10)** www. .... .com

Questions 11 – 15

For each question, choose the correct answer.

You will hear Elena and her brother Paul talking about going to stay at their grandparents' farm.

11   Who will drive them to the farm?

   A   their mum   ☐

   B   their grandfather   ☐

   C   their aunt   ☐

12   How does Elena feel about the journey?

   A   excited about what they'll see on the way   ☐

   B   surprised that it'll take a long time   ☐

   C   worried they might be bored   ☐

13   What will Paul take with him?

   A   something to play   ☐

   B   something to read   ☐

   C   something to listen to   ☐

14   On the farm, Elena and Paul are hoping to

   A   try some cooking.   ☐

   B   go horse riding.   ☐

   C   do some work.   ☐

15   Which present will they give their grandparents?

   A   a picture   ☐

   B   some chocolates   ☐

   C   some flowers   ☐

Part 4

For each question, choose the correct answer.

_____

16   You will hear a girl leaving a phone message for her mum.
     What hasn't the girl done?

     A   bought what she needed in town

     B   checked the times of the buses home

     C   told her mum she'll be late

17   You will hear two friends talking about a nature programme on TV.
     What did they both think about it?

     A   It wasn't very interesting.

     B   It didn't teach them anything.

     C   It wasn't long enough.

18   You will hear a boy talking to his mum about a trip to the city stadium.
     What's his problem?

     A   He's lost something.

     B   He's made a mistake about something.

     C   He's going to be late for something.

19   You will hear a girl talking to a friend about going to a museum.
     Why did she visit the museum?

     A   to do some drawing

     B   to visit a special exhibition

     C   to collect information for school

20   You will hear a boy phoning his friend.
     Where is the boy now?

     A   in a small shop

     B   in an outdoor market

     C   in a department store

Part 5

Questions 21 – 25

For each question, choose the correct answer.

You will hear Josh talking to his grandma about talks by his classmates on their favourite films. What was each classmate's favourite film about?

Example:

0   brother $\boxed{A}$

People

21   Alex   ☐

22   Bella   ☐

23   Henry   ☐

24   Sandie   ☐

25   Jed   ☐

What the film was about

A   an animal

B   an artist

C   a family

D   a forest

E   a game

F   a musical instrument

G   a plane journey

H   a sport

Part I (3–4 minutes)

Phase I

The examiner will ask you and your partner some questions about yourself.

To both candidates	Good morning / afternoon / evening.
	I'm ...., and this is ....
(*Candidate A*)	What's your name?
(*Candidate B*)	And what's your name?

(*Candidate B*)
B, how old are you? ....
Where do you come from? ....

Where do you live? ....

Thank you.

(*Candidate B*)
A, how old are you? ....
Where do you come from? ....

Where do you live? ....

Thank you.

> **Extra help questions**
>
> Are you from (Spain, etc.)?
> Do you live in … (name of district / town, etc.)?
>
>
>
> Are you from (Spain, etc.)?
> Do you live in … (name of district / town, etc.)?

Now, let's talk about **birthdays**.

A, how old will you be on your next birthday?

And, what do you usually do on your birthday?

B, do you usually have a party for your birthday?

And what kind of presents do you like getting on your birthday?

Extended response
Now, **A**, tell me about what you did on your last birthday.

Extra questions

When is your birthday?

Do you go out on your birthday?

Do friends come to your house for your birthday?

What do people give you on your birthday?

Extra questions
What did you eat?
Did you have a cake?
Who did you spend the day with?

Now, let's talk about **reading**.

B, when do you read?..........

And, what do you enjoy reading?..........

A, what is your favourite book?..........

And, what do you read on screen?..........

Extended response
Now, **B**, tell me something about the last book you read.

Extra help questions

Do you read before you go to sleep?

Do you like reading comics?

Do you enjoy reading stories?

Do you read things on your laptop or tablet?

Extra questions
Who wrote the book?
Was it a true story?
Did you enjoy reading it?

Part 2 (5–6 minutes)

Phase 1 (3–4 minutes)

Now, in this part of the test, you are going to talk together.

[Turn to the pictures on page 51]

Here are some pictures that show **different things you can do at the beach.**

Do you like these different beach activities? Say why or why not.

I'll say that again. Do you like these different beach activities? Say why or why not.

All right? Now, talk together.

🕐 *1–2 minutes*

The examiner will ask you at least one question each:

Do you think ...
... swimming in the sea is nice?
... having a picnic on the beach is exciting?
... playing volleyball is fun?
... surfing in the sea is difficult?
... taking photos on the beach is interesting?

So **A**, which of these activities do you like best?
And you, **B**, which of these activities do you like best?

🕐 *1–2 minutes*

Thank you.

Extra questions

Why?/ Why not?
What do **you** think?

Part 2

Phase 2 (*up to 2 minutes*)

Now, do you enjoy going to the beach, **B**? … (Why?/Why not?)

And what about you, **A**? (Do you enjoy going to the beach?) …
(Why?/Why not?)

Where is your favourite place to go and spend some time
outside, **A**? … (Why)

And what about you, **B**? (Where is your favourite place to go and spend some time
outside?) … (Why?)

🕒 *1–2 minutes*

Thank you. That is the end of the test.

VISUALS BANK

Part 2

Do you like these different kinds of TV programmes?

Part 2

Do you like these different beach activities?

SPEAKING BANK

You take the Speaking test with a partner, and there are two examiners. One examiner speaks to you, and the other examiner just listens. There are two parts to the test. Each part has two phases. The whole test takes 8–10 minutes.

Exam help

✓ These questions are always the same, and you already know the answers, so practise answering them clearly and confidently.

✓ Remember, you only need to give short answers to these questions.

Part I Phase I

You answer simple questions about your name, age and where you live.

Useful language

Giving personal information
My name's …
I'm … years old
I come from …
I live in the city centre.
I live in a city/town/village.

Exam help

✓ You can give short answers to these questions but when the examiner says, 'Tell me something about …' you should give a longer answer.

✓ Always try to think of something interesting to say.

✓ Think about the tense you're going to use. The question may be about the present, the past or the future.

✓ Speak clearly.

✓ If you don't understand, ask the examiner to repeat.

✓ These questions are always the same, and you already know the answers, so practise answering them clearly and confidently.

✓ Remember, you only need to give short answers to these questions.

Part I Phase 2

In this part of the test, you answer some personal questions about two different things, for example your family, your school, your daily life or what you do in your free time.

Useful language

Likes and dislikes
I enjoy … because …
On Tuesdays I play basketball/go swimming.
On Saturdays I go shopping/meet my friends …
I like/love/enjoy …
I don't like/hate …
I'm good/brilliant at …
I'm OK/not good at …
It's amazing/brilliant/cool!
My favourite … is … because …

Asking the examiner to repeat
Sorry, I don't understand.
Could you say that again, please?
Can you repeat that, please?

Practice activity 1

Fill the gaps with some information about yourself.

My name's ....
I'm .... years old.
I live in ....
I come from ....
There are .... people in my family.
My favourite sport is .... because ....
I like .... music best because ....
Last year I went to .... on holiday. It was fun because ....

Practice activity 2

Complete the sentences with a word from the box.

at	because	go	listen	not	to

1 I usually see my friends .... the weekend.

2 I often .... to music with my friends.

3 I sometimes go .... my friend's house.

4 I .... to school by bus.

5 I don't really enjoy my journey .... it's quite boring.

6 It's .... easy to travel around my city because it's very busy!

Practice activity 3

Tick (✓) the sentences you could say if an examiner says, 'Tell me something about your best friend.'

1 I met my best friend at football club. ☐

2 It's good to have best friends. ☐

3 My brother's best friend's called Rob. ☐

4 My best friend lives in my street. ☐

5 My favourite TV show is about two best friends. ☐

6 I go to the same school as my best friend. ☐

Part 2 Phase I

Comparing, describing and expressing opinions.

The examiner gives you and your partner some pictures to look at.

The examiner asks you and your partner if you like or dislike the different activities, things or places shown in the pictures. You reply and you also have to give reasons for your opinions.

You and your partner should talk together about the pictures.

Useful language

Saying you like something and giving a reason

I like quiz programmes. I think they're interesting.
I like them because I love answering the questions.
I always love going to the beach because I love the sea!
I really enjoy swimming in the sea. I think it's good fun.

Saying you dislike something and giving a reason

In my opinion, the cinema is boring. That's why I don't like it.
I don't like it because, for me, the films are often too long.
And I don't really enjoy restaurants. I prefer picnics outside.
I don't like sports programmes. I like playing sport, not watching it.

Exam help

✓ Remember you have to talk to your partner in this part.
✓ Look at your partner when you speak to her/him.
✓ Look at each picture and say if you like or dislike what it shows.
✓ Give a reason for your opinion.
✓ Sometimes you can talk about a picture first and sometimes your partner can talk about a picture first.
✓ Talk for as long as you can. The examiner will tell you when to stop.
✓ Don't stop talking if you don't know a word. Try to use other words to say what you want, or move on to talk about something else.

Part 2 Phase 2

The examiner asks you and your partner one or two questions on the same topic as Phase 1.

Exam help

✓ Always listen carefully when the examiner asks your partner a question first because the examiner will then ask, 'And what about you?'
✓ If you forget the question, ask the examiner to say it again.
✓ Use the vocabulary and grammar that you have learned.
✓ Listen carefully to the instructions.
✓ If you're not sure what to do, ask the examiner to say it again.
✓ Speak clearly so that both examiners can hear what you say.

Practice activity 4

Complete the sentences with a word or phrase from the box.

| enjoy | for me | opinion | prefer | really | think |

1 I .... like team sports.

2 In my .... museums are really interesting.

3 I .... that restaurants are a good place to go with your family.

4 I don't really .... watching comedy programmes.

5 I don't enjoy going for long walks. I .... cycling.

6 I don't like the summer because, ..., the weather's too hot.

Practice activity 5

Match 1–6 with A–F.

1 My favourite activity is surfing because   **A** I like all kinds of art.

2 I prefer watching sport than   **B** I prefer going to the cinema with friends.

3 I like going to restaurants best because   **C** I love being in the sea.

4 I enjoy painting and drawing;   **D** I love food!

5 I like rock music, but   **E** I don't enjoy listening to classical music.

6 I enjoy watching films with my family, but   **F** playing sport.

Practice activity 6

Put the words in the correct order to make useful sentences and questions.

1 your question. / I'm / I / understand / sorry, / didn't

....

2 you / the question, / please? / Could / repeat

....

3 that / Could / say / again, / you / please?

....

4 I / the question. / didn't / hear / sorry, / I'm

....

5 not / I / sure / that word. / understand / I'm

....

6 mean? / What / that / does

....

WRITING BANK

Part 6 a short message

In Part 6, you have to write a short message. You read an email or information about a situation. You have to answer three questions about it then you write an email or message of 25 words or more.

Test 1, Part 6, (page 16)

Your friend Lee was sick on Friday and now wants to know about the class geography project.

Write an email to Lee.

Say:

- **what** he has to write about

- **how** much he has to write

- **when** he needs to complete it by.

Write **25 words** or more.

Sample answer

start the email in a friendly way

this is the first content point (telling Lee what he has to write about)

this is the second content point (how much he has to write)

this is the third content point (when he needs to complete it by)

finish your email in a friendly way

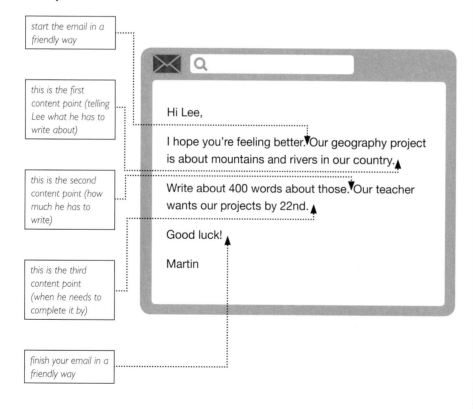

Hi Lee,

I hope you're feeling better. Our geography project is about mountains and rivers in our country.

Write about 400 words about those. Our teacher wants our projects by 22nd.

Good luck!

Martin

Useful language

Starting an email

Hi,
Great news! I've got a new bike.
How are you?
Guess what? I'm going on a school trip to France!

Ending an email

Have a great weekend!
Please write to me soon.
See you next week!
Love

Exam help

✓ Read all the questions carefully so that you understand the situation.

✓ Read the questions and think about the grammar you need to use in your answers (e.g. if you read, *Who did you see at the weekend?* you will write, *I saw …*).

✓ Remember to write in complete sentences and use the correct punctuation (capital letters, full stops, etc.).

✓ Use friendly language.

✓ Make sure that you answer all three questions.

✓ Start your email with a friendly greeting, for example, *Hi.*

✓ Finish your email in a friendly way.

✓ Check your email for grammar or spelling mistakes.

✓ Write at least 25 words.

Practice activity 1

Correct the punctuation in this email.

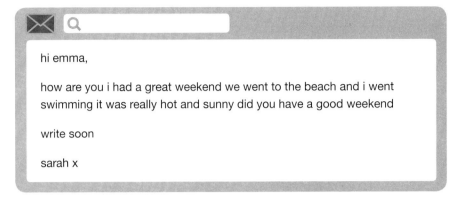

hi emma,

how are you i had a great weekend we went to the beach and i went swimming it was really hot and sunny did you have a good weekend

write soon

sarah x

Practice activity 2

Complete the sentences with a preposition from the box.

at	in	on	to	with	by

1 The club starts .... 7:30 pm.

2 We'll travel to the cinema .... train.

3 Do you want to play tennis .... Wednesday?

4 My birthday's .... June and I'm having a party.

5 I'm going .... the park. Would you like to come?

6 My dad's taking me to the football match. Do you want to come .... us?

Practice activity 3

Put the words in the correct order.

1 you / go to / Would / the sports centre? / like to

   ....

2 in the park / want to / at 3 pm? / Do / meet / you

   ....

3 next weekend. / to / going / London / I'm

   ....

4 the school trip? / you / on / going / Are

   ....

5 tomorrow? / my house / Can / to / you / come

   ....

6 your party. / I / I'm / can't / to / sorry, / come

   ....

In Part 7 you have to write a short story based on three pictures.

Test 1, Part 7, (page 17)

Look at the three pictures. Write the story shown in the pictures.
Write **35 words** or more.

Useful language

You can write your story using present or past tenses. If you want to make your story better, you need to write it in the past tense and …

- use verbs in the past tense (e.g. *was, ran, saw, opened*) because the story happened in the past.
- use words that link the actions in the past (e.g. *after that, later, when*) to make your story easy to follow.
- use a variety of adjectives and expressions (e.g. *terrible, afraid, surprised, suddenly*) to add interest to your story.

Exam help

- ✓ Describe each picture.
- ✓ Say who you can see in each picture and what the people are/were doing.
- ✓ Make sure that your story has a beginning, a middle and an end.
- ✓ Say where the story happened.
- ✓ Include words that explain when things happened (e.g. *Later*).
- ✓ Include words like *because* and *so* if possible.
- ✓ Include some adjectives.
- ✓ Check your work for grammar or spelling mistakes.
- ✓ Write at least 35 words.

Sample answer

Use different verb tenses to describe what happened.

Use linking words such as 'and' to join your ideas.

Use time words like 'then' to show what order things happened.

Two girls are riding their bikes beside a lake. It's a nice day. One girl is wearing sunglasses, and the other girl has a big hat. Then the girl's hat falls off – into the water! They stop their bikes and the girl picks up her hat. It's very wet. She's sad.

Use a variety of adjectives.

Say how the person or people in the story are feeling.

WRITING BANK

Practice activity 4

Complete the sentences with *and, but, because* or *so*.

1 I switched the light on .... I heard a loud noise.

2 Mark was hungry .... he had a biscuit.

3 The girl bought a new skirt .... a new top.

4 They felt sick .... they ate too much food.

5 I didn't like the film .... I didn't watch all of it.

6 He likes cooking .... he doesn't like sport.

7 Adam's got a brother .... a sister.

8 I wanted to buy an ice cream .... I didn't have any money.

Practice activity 5

Choose the correct adjectives.

1 We laughed a lot because it was a very **fun / funny** story.

2 Kirsty thought the film was very **boring / bored**.

3 The party was **brilliant / terrible!** Everyone had a great time.

4 The concert was so **noisy / quiet!** I couldn't hear what my friends were saying.

5 My friend Oliver sang in front of the whole school. I think he's very **careful / brave**.

6 Everyone knew the actor. He was very **famous / favourite**.

7 Liam was **alone / worried** because he couldn't find his keys.

8 The man couldn't lift the box because it was very **heavy / hungry**.

Practice activity 6

Choose the correct form of the verbs in the story.

Joe **(1) gets / was getting** ready for school. He **(2)** *was* **having / had** one shoe but **(3) can't / couldn't** find his other shoe. He **(4) looked / 'll look** in the cupboard under the stairs. His shoe **(5) wasn't being / wasn't** there. Suddenly he **(6)** *was* **seeing / saw** it. His cat **(7) was sitting / sits** on it! Joe **(8) laughed / laughs**.

A2 KEY for Schools Top 20 Questions

1 What is the format of the A2 KEY for Schools exam, and are all the papers taken on the same day?
There are three papers:
➤ Reading and Writing (1 hour)
Listening (about 30 minutes) Speaking (9–10 minutes)
Papers 1 and 2 are always taken on the same day. The Speaking test may be taken on the same day or on a different day.

2 How is the A2 KEY for Schools exam different from the A2 KEY exam?
➤ KET for Schools follows the same format as KET. The difference is that the content and topics in KET for Schools are more suitable for the interests and experiences of younger people.

3 What level is the A2 KEY for Schools exam?
➤ The KEY for Schools exam is aligned to the Council of Europe Common European Framework for Reference (CEFR) and is level A2 in the CEFR.

4 Is the A2 KEY for schools exam suitable for teenagers from any culture?
➤ Yes. All tasks are written to avoid any cultural bias.

5 What are the grade ranges for the A2 KEY for Schools exam?
➤ There are four grades with fixed values: Pass with merit = 85–100%
Pass = 70–84%
A1 = 45–69%
Fail = 44% and below

6 Do I have to pass each paper in order to pass the exam?
➤ No. Each paper doesn't have a pass or fail mark. The final mark a candidate gets in KET for Schools is an average mark obtained by adding the marks for all three papers together.

7 What mark do I need to get to pass the exam overall?
➤ To achieve a pass in the A2 KEY for Schools exam a candidate must receive a minimum of 70% as an overall average.

8 When can I use pens or pencils in the exam?
➤ In the A2 KEY for Schools exam, a candidate must use pencil in all papers.

9 If I write entirely in capital letters, does this affect my score?
➤ No. Candidates are not penalised for writing in capitals in the exam.

10 Am I allowed to use a dictionary?
➤ No.

11 Is correct spelling important in Paper 1 (Reading and Writing)?
➤ It is important only in Parts 5, 6 and 7.

12 Is correct spelling important in Paper 2 (Listening)?
➤ It is important only in Part 2.

13 In Paper 1 (Reading and Writing) will extra time be given for me to transfer my answers to the answer sheet?
➤ No. You must transfer them in the 1 hour you are given to complete the exam in.

14 In Paper 2 (Listening) will extra time be given for me to transfer my answers to the answer sheet?
➤ Yes. You will be given some time at the end of the test for this.

15 How many times will I hear each recording in Paper 2 (Listening)?
➤ You will hear each recording twice.

16 Can I ask any questions if I don't understand something in Papers 1 (Reading and Writing) and 2 (Listening)?
➤ The only questions you can ask are those that relate to the rules of the exam. For example, the time you have, where to write your name or your answers, completing the answer sheet, whether or not you can use a pen, etc. You cannot ask for any help with the test items themselves.

17 Can I ask any questions if I don't understand something in Paper 3 (Speaking)?
➤ Yes. You can ask the examiner to repeat a question in Part 1 and to repeat the instructions in Part 2. If you still don't understand, tell the examiner you don't understand. You can ask your partner to repeat or clarify when they are asking you questions or answering your questions in Part 2.

18 In Paper 3 (Speaking), do I have to go in with another student? Can I choose my partner?
➤ You cannot be examined alone. You will usually be examined with one other candidate, but if you are one of the last candidates to be examined and there is an odd number of candidates on the day, you may be examined in a group of three. In some smaller centres you may be able to choose your partner, but in bigger centres this may not be possible.

19 In Paper 3 (Speaking), is it a good idea for me to prepare what I am going to say in Part 1?
➤ It's a good idea to practise saying your name, spelling your surname and talking about yourself (your family, school, school subjects, hobbies, etc.). It is important that you answer the examiner's questions and that you do so naturally, so listen carefully and think about the questions you have been asked. If you give a prepared speech you may not answer the examiner's question. You will lose marks if your answers are irrelevant.

20 In Paper 3 (Speaking), what if I can't understand my partner in Part 2 or if he/she can't understand me?
➤ If there is a communication breakdown between you and your partner in Part 2, try to solve the problem between you. For example, ask your partner for clarification or to repeat a question or an answer, or help your partner if necessary. You will be given credit for helping your partner if he/she is having difficulty.

Pearson Education Limited

KAO TWO,
KAO Park
Hockham Way,
Harlow, Essex,
CM17 9SR
England and Associated Companies throughout the world.

www.pearsonELT.com/goldexperience

First published 2018
ISBN: 978-1-292-19520-9
Set in Helvetica Neue LT 10pt and Gill Sans 9pt
Printed by Neografia, in Slovakia

Picture Credits
The publisher would like to thank the following for their kind permission to reproduce their photographs:

123RF.com: Oleksandr Pekur 38, Paulo Resende 12, Roman Mikhailiuk 36, gonewiththewind 11; **Beehive Illustration Agency:** Jérôme Brasseur 17, 20, 21, 41, 42, 43, 52, 53, 60; Pearson Education Ltd: Studio 8 11; **Shutterstock.com:** Ann Worthy 11, Blend Images 35, MVPhoto 14, Samuel Borges Photography 35, Tracy Whiteside 35.

Cover Image: 123RF.com: mihtiander
All other images © Pearson Education

Every effort has been made to trace the copyright holders and we apologise in advance for any unintentional omissions. We would be pleased to insert the appropriate acknowledgement in any subsequent edition of this publication